Bibliography :
Our main sources for this booklet were :

Arsène Alexandre : «Le jardin de Monet »
Le Figaro, 9 août 1901

Maurice Kahn : «Le jardin de Claude Monet »
Le Temps, 7 juin 1904

Louis Vauxcelles : «Un après-midi chez Claude Monet »
L'Art et les Artistes, 15 mai 1909

Roger Marx : « Les Nymphéas de M. Claude Monet »
La Gazette des Beaux-Arts, 1909

Gustave Geffroy : « Claude Monet, sa vie, son temps, son œuvre »
Paris, 1912

Georges Truffaut : « Le jardin de Claude Monet »
Jardinage 87, novembre 1924

Georges Clemenceau : « Claude Monet - Les Nymphéas »
Paris 1928

Jean-Pierre Hoschedé : « Claude Monet, ce mal connu »
Genève, 1960

René Gimpel : « Journal d'un collectionneur, marchand de tableaux»
Paris, 1963

Paulette Howard Johnston : « Une visite à Giverny en 1924 »
L'Œil, mars 1969

John Rewald : « The history of Impressionism »
New York, 1973

Claire Joyes, « Monet at Giverny »
London, 1975

Daniel Wildenstein : « Monet's years at Giverny - Beyond Impressionism »
Metropolitan Mus. of Art, 1978

Cover :
Claude Monet's House
The Water Garden

The plan page 24 of Claude Monet's property at Giverny was originally drawn for the exhibition held at the Metropolitan Museum of Art entitled : "Monet's Years at Giverny Beyond Impressionism."

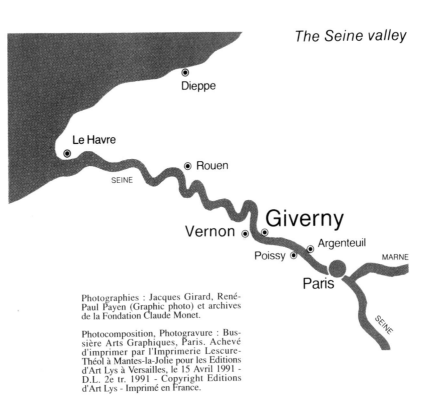

The Seine valley

Photographies : Jacques Girard, René-Paul Payen (Graphic photo) et archives de la Fondation Claude Monet.

Photocomposition, Photogravure : Bussière Arts Graphiques, Paris. Achevé d'imprimer par l'Imprimerie Lescure-Théol à Mantes-la-Jolie pour les Editions d'Art Lys à Versailles, le 15 Avril 1991 - D.L. 2e tr. 1991 - Copyright Editions d'Art Lys - Imprimé en France.

Claude Monet's immense number of paintings belong to many different museums and private collections. Visitors to Giverny will find them presented in various works, in particular in L'Hommage à Claude Monet, published in spring 1980 for one of the finest exhibitions held by the Musées Nationaux at the Grand Palais in Paris. It seemed unnecessary to include reproductions of paintings in this catalogue which is intented to reveal the home and gardens, the universe familiar to a great painter.

Photographs alone were chosen as illustrations, in the humble hope that the master, himself an ardent lover of photography, would not have rejected this choice.

1

Claude Monet
at Giverny
1910-1914

A VISIT TO GIVERNY

Translation by Bronia Fuchs

GERALD VAN DER KEMP
Membre de l'Institut
Conservateur de la Fondation Claude Monet

Introduction

Giverny ! A charming village spread out along a hillside not far from Vernon... Giverny, a name now famous because of the residence chosen by a great artist. It was there that Claude Monet decided to settle in April 1883. "I am filled with delight, Giverny is a splendid spot for me...", he wrote, scarcely one month after moving there. Before visiting his home, his garden and his pools, one should say something of the painter's life and his sources of inspiration.

Claude Monet came into the world in Paris in 1840. He spent his childhood and youth at Le Havre where, in the years between 1858 and 1862, he met the painters Eugène Boudin and Jongkind, who introduced him to the pleasures of painting in the open air, directly from nature. On going to Paris to study, he met Renoir, Sisley and Bazille. He admired Manet and worked side by side with Courbet at Trouville. In London he discovered Turner in 1871 and it was at this time that he began to admire and collect Japanese engravings. He settled in Argenteuil between 1872 and 1878 and began to work on the water in a boat converted into a studio. He suffered a period of extreme hardship during these years, when he married Camille who bore him a son, Jean. His works were exhibited in 1874, 1876, 1877 and 1882 and called "Impression, soleil levant".

In 1876, Ernest Hoschedé, a businessman and collector, invited him to the château of Rottembourg in Montgeron. He became a family friend and met Edouard Manet, Carolus Duran and many others there. Ernest Hoschedé went bankrupt and fled to Belgium in 1877. Madame Hoschedé and Madame Monet decided to spend the summer of 1878 together. They rented a house in Vétheuil but Claude Monet was completely lacking in enthusiasm about it. His wife gave birth to a second son, Michel, and she herself died of tuberculosis in 1879, a painful loss for Monet. Alice Hoschedé then decided to help Claude by bringing up his two children together with her own. They left for Poissy, which Monet hated and, when the lease was up in April 1883, he visited the outer areas of Vexin in search of other accomodation. From the doorway of the little train between Vernon and Gasny he discovered Giverny, where he moved with Alice Hoschedé and the children. To begin with they lived in an inn and then rented a house from Louis-Joseph Singeot. It was here that Claude Monet settled permanently. The property spread over almost two and a half acres and sloped down towards the bottom of the village. At the lower end is the "chemin du Roy", along which ran a small local railway connecting Vernon and Gasny, and at the upper

limit was the "rue de l'Amsicourt", now called the " rue Claude Monet". The house stands beside the road and looks onto a large orchard. There was a single-storey barn to the left of the house as one comes from the garden. Monet immediately made this his drawing room and studio, where he loved to sit and smoke while examining in minute detail the canvases painted in the open air.

Preceding pages : hollyhocks and poppies near the house.

The central pathway bordered with nasturtiums.

The rose season :
rambler roses
of pale shades intertwine
on the metal
archways
of the central pathway
and the trellis
above the railing
along the front
of the house while
rose bushes bloom
in fiery tones
to the east
of the Clos Normand.

View of the house,
looking west.

He had flowers planted in his garden to enable him to paint in either fine or rainy weather. Every day, untiringly, he reproduced on his canvases the fields, the trees and the river Seine. He even bought an island for this purpose, the "île aux Orties", on which he owned a hut and a boat studio. The daughter of the painter Helleu, Paulette Howard Johnston, describes him as being "of medium height, stout, with a thick neck and standing squarely on his legs, his hair cut very close with, however, a very long white beard. He wore a suit of a thick, greyish woollen fabric, trousers fastened at the ankles, a white shirt with finely folded cuffs which just showed under the sleeves of his high-buttoned jacket... He had a clear, ringing voice... he was extremely simple and natural ; his direct way of speaking inspired confidence and although he gave the impression at first sight of being rather peasant-like, this vanished as soon as he began to speak : one quickly realized just how refined his mind was". Lucien Descaves noted that he liked good living, drinking his wine pure, and could bear water only in small doses after his morning drink of chocolate. However, he smoked forty cigarettes a day... mostly in the open air and threw them away half-smoked. He always had several canvases underway due to the changing light. He was obses-

A clump of
hollyhocks along
a path
to the east
of the
Clos Normand wrapped
in the haze
of a summer evening
as the rain
draws near.

Along
the central
pathway sunflowers
face the morning
light while
bees swarm
around.

Chiaroscuro effects on
the eastern paths of the Clos Normand.

Snapdragons and
hybrid lilies

sed and tortured by his painting. He painted furiously and,
very often dissatisfied, des-
troyed his work. During his
crises, his family created an
atmosphere of respectful si-
lence around him. But when a
painting was successful, he
once more became cheerful,
approachable and the most
pleasant man in the world.

He would rise at five o'clock
each morning and wander
along the paths of Giverny, the
banks of the river Epte and the
rows of poplars, in the fields
red with poppies and along the
banks of the Seine. It was at
Giverny that he became the
forerunner of modern painting. Disregarding all the ten-
dencies of his time, the Nabis,
Pointillists, Fauvists and
Cubists, he obstinately plou-
ghed his own furrow. "The
subject is of secondary impor-
tance to me ; what I want to
reproduce is what exists between the subject and me".
"The subject of his painting is
not light and shade, but the
painting placed in light and
shade". In this way, the subject
disappeared from his paintings at the end of his life, thus
heralding the arrival of abstract art.

It was at Giverny that he began
his well-known "Séries" which
later made him famous. He
executed the series of twenty-
five "Haystacks" between 1888
and 1891. In 1892, he exhibited a set of twenty-four Poplars at the Durand-Ruel gallery ; from 1892 to 1898, he

10

painted the series of Cathedrals, "Matinées sur la Seine" and then the Japanese Bridge, Wistarias and Water Lilies with their interplay of sky, clouds, grass and flowers. All is reflected on a surface which is itself illusory. And finally came the apotheosis with the large decorative panels of water lilies, called the "Décorations des Nymphéas", in which shapes gradually give way to a triumph of colour.

At the time of his move to Giverny he was in dire financial straits and the art dealer Durand-Ruel, through his financial support, helped Monet and his large family to live comfortably. As he became more widely known and his canvases began to sell well, Monet decided to buy the house for the sum of 22,000 francs. He then altered the garden, constructed three green houses and, on the other side of the "chemin du Roy", bought a plot of land on which, after countless administrative difficulties, he succeeded, in 1895, in creating the famous pool and built the Japanese Bridge after an engraving. In 1892, he married Alice Hoschedé who, respected and respectable, brought an element of stability into his life. Cézanne, Renoir, Rodin, Sisley, Pissarro, Matisse, John Singer Sargent, the critic Gustave Geffroy and Octave Mirbeau visited him there. He became an intimate friend of Georges Clemenceau, who sho-

As a whole
Claude Monet's work
at Giverny
has two successive
and complementary
features.
First, the gardens
created with patience
over several decades
should be
considered as
a work of art
in themselves.
Conceived by
a painter
with a passion
for horticulture,
these gardens
inspired the famous
expression
"a painting executed
on nature itself".
Second, from the
countless motifs
which could be
painted and
little by little
surrounded the house
and studios,
the pictorial world
as displayed by
the master's works
now scattered
throughout the
world's museums
and collections
was born.

Cleome
and foxglove

The Japanese
Bridge

Right, chiaroscuro effect
on the shores of the pond.

wered him with admiration and affection until his death. He neither understood nor could bear Gauguin's painting but liked that of Vuillard — "a very good eye" — and Maurice Denis — "a very fine talent". After lunch, he liked showing his friends his private collection on the first floor of his house. In 1899, he had a second studio built particularly for its good light, to the left of the garden, in front of the green houses. He also had a garage constructed as well as a dark room for photography and two bedrooms. During this period, art dealers vied with each other for his clientele. He entrusted his canvases to Boussod and Valadon, to the Bernheim brothers and to Georges Petit, and Durand-Ruel suffered cruelly because of this. However, it was at the latter's gallery that he exhibited a magnificent series of Water Lilies (1900) and became famous throughout France, England and the United States. In 1899, too, his daughter-in-law, Suzanne, died, an irreparable loss for her mother. Exhibitions and trips to Norway, London, Italy and the coast of Normandy followed in rapid succession. In May 1911, the death of his wife left him completely at a loss.

Fortunately, he still had his daughter-in-law, Blanche and Georges Clemenceau. His son, Jean, Blanche's husband, died in 1914. Completely shattered,

Monet began to suffer from cataracts ; Clemenceau urged him to press on with his artistic research. He therefore began to dream of creating the "Décorations des Nymphéas", for which he built a huge and unsightly studio from 1914 to 1915, at the top of the garden, on the left. His gigantic task was begun in 1916 and, after various interruptions, ended with a magnificent series of canvases being donated to France on 12th April 1922.

In January and July 1923, he underwent operations on his right eye. He died depressed, hopeless and exhausted on 5th December 1926.

Michel Monet, his second son, with whom relations had been strained, was his father's heir. He lived in Sorel, Eure-et-Loir, but occasionally came to Giverny, where everything had remained as it was, devotedly watched over by his sister-in-law, Blanche. She looked after the property and gardens and kept alive the memory of the master until her death after the 1940 war. The head gardener, Lebret, also died and the care of the property was left to an assistant gardener. Gradually, the garden fell into neglect, most of the paintings were sold and, on returning from a visit to Giverny, Michel, then aged 88, was injured in a car accident and died on 19 January 1966. In his will, Michel left the entire property to the Académie des Beaux-Arts.

Appointed Curator of Giverny

by my colleagues in 1977, I immediately undertook the preservation of the gardens, with the help of funds from the Institut and donations from the Conseil Général de l'Eure, the Préfecture de l'Eure and the Association "Richesses de l'Eure". I then took on a head gardener, M. Vahé, a brilliant student from the Ecole Nationale d'Horticulture.

Georges Truffaut, whom the master had invited to dine with him, often visited him at Giverny. He was accompanied by a young man, M. André Devillers, who later became general manager of the Georges Truffaut Company. With the help of M. Thibaudin, he was kind enough to give generously the benefit of his experience and memories. I am also greatly indebted to M. Toulgouat, (Claude Monet's great-nephew), and his wife for a long and detailed study of a theoretical reconstitution of the gardens. Finally, André de Vilmorin kindly helped me with his expert opinion. Let me express my thanks to all these people. Through them, and the work and talent of M. Vahé, a miracle has taken place : the garden is at last in its original state again.

Once the funds donated by the Institut were depleted, my wife, (an American, and President of the Versailles Foundation), and I left for the United States where we were authorized to accept tax-deductible donations for Giverny

The painter's boat moored to
the south bank of the pond.
Preceding pages : chiaroscuro effects
in the clumps to the east
of the Clos Normand.

A glimpse of the little bridge straddling
the arm of the river Epte
which supplies water to the pool,
seen through azalea bushes
on the north shore.

from Americans through the Versailles Foundation.

A great friend of France and a fervent admirer of claude Monet, Mrs Lila Acheson Wallace, generoulsy made a very important donation. Other friends from New-York, Washington, Chicago, Palm Beach, New Orleans, Dallas, Houston, Los Angeles, San Francisco and, naturally, from France, also offered us their financial support. Ambassador Walter Annenberg spontaneously gave a large sum to connect the gardens and pools with a tunnel (under the new road which has, alas, replaced the former "chemin du Roy"). Each year the Claude Monet Foundation welcomes many visitors from all over the world. As Claude Monet's fame spread, American painters gradually moved to Giverny from 1890 onwards.

The first of these was Theodore Robinson, introduced to Claude Monet by a friend ; he moved from Fontainebleau to settle at Giverny.

Another American artist, Metcalf, moved into an inn called "L'Auberge Baudy" and was invited to dinner by Claude Monet. Then came the invasion which drove Monet to despair : the belgian, Théo van Rysselberghe, William Hart, Miss Wheeler, the Czech, Radinsky, the Norwegian, Thornley, the Scot, Watson, the Americans, Bec kwith, Theodore Butler, Johnstone, Finn, Perry and Lila Cabott

View of the house facing east in subdued morning light. In the foreground, a cluster of peonies.

In a border to the north of the Clos Normand, floral arrangement seen against the light of the setting sun.

Perry, Hart Friescke, Mary Cassatt, Rosc, etc., and the inn became the "Hôtel Baudy". After Claude Monet's death, a number of surrealists also settled at Giverny.

Many abstract painters have spoken of the influence of Monet's last canvases on their own work. For them, the "Water Lilies" are not minor decorative "post-impressionist" works but rather go a step beyond impressionism. They are a vertical interpretation of a horizontal scene — the surface of water — a rejection of all traditional limits. The interplay of reflections alone recreates all the surrounding nature, the colours explode to the detriment of all figurative form. "They gave to painting a fantastic strength and brilliance. But, unconsciously, the object, as an indispensable element of a painting, was also discredited", wrote Kandinsky. However, one should also quote André Masson and Joan Mitchelle and recognize Monet's influence in the paintings of many contemporary artists, such as Pollock, Sam Francis, Judith Reigl, etc.

Claude Monet may thus be considered not only as one of the greatest painters of his time but also as a precursor of modern art.

The Clos Normand on a summer morning.

In the clumps at dusk.

The Gardens

Georges Clemenceau, speaking of his friend Claude Monet, used to say that "his garden was his studio". Monet was indeed very fondly attached to it, and during his last moments the garden alone filled his thoughts. In fact, the garden features two aspects of Monet's taste : on one side, what he called the Clos Normand, on the other the Water Garden surrounding the pools.

A the Clos Normand
1 The house
2 The second studio
3 The Water Lily studio
4 The green houses

B The Water Garden
a Water inlet to the pool
b Water Lily pool
c Landing stage
d Japanese Bridge

C Underpass connecting the gardens

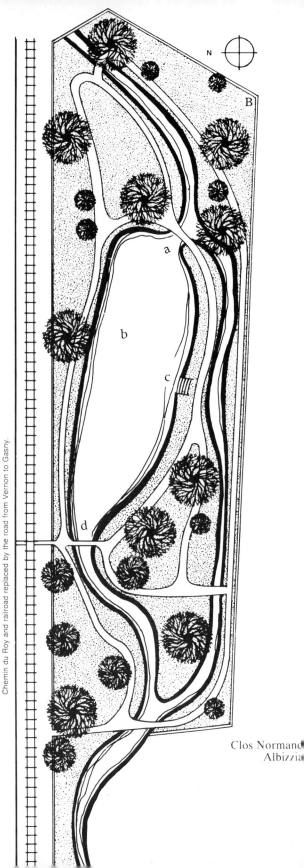

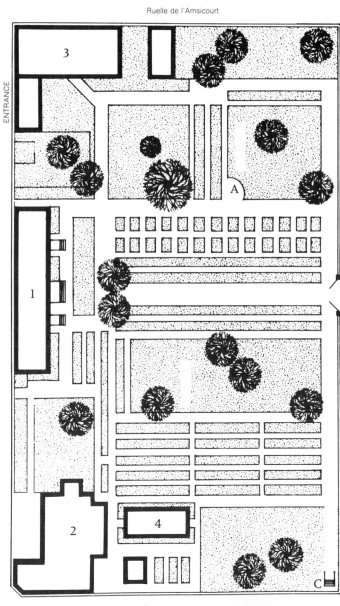

Clos Normand
Albizzia

Ruelle de l'Amsicourt

PARKING AREA

ENTRANCE

Rue Claude-Monet

VERNON

Chemin du Roy and railroad replaced by the road from Vernon to Gasny.

The *Clos Normand* is designed in the French style. It lies in front of the house, intersected by paths running in straight lines, and is ordered despite the profusion, variety and brilliance of the

colours which change with the seasons. Claude Monet's love of gardening was enhanced through his friend ship with Caillebotte, at Argenteuil. Wherever he lived, he had a small garden, at Ville d'Avray, Louveciennes, Argenteuil and Vétheuil.

At Giverny, he at last owned an orchard, through the middle of which ran a large pathway flanked by two wide flower-beds and

Claude Monet's art is based on the observation of nature. The gardens, created on his property over several years, became a recurrent theme of his painting around 1900, (before becoming its only subject at the end of his life). Although the landscapes of the Water Garden are the best-known, the « Clos Normand », with its straight lines and different varieties of flowers blossoming according to the seasons, provided Monet with subjects for a large number of paintings.

ending at the "chemin du Roy". In the flower-beds grew spruces, yew-trees and large clumps of box-tree. After endless painful arguments with Alice, he kept the two yews in front of the house and replaced the spruces and box-trees with metal archways and, under the arcade of roses, the central pathway was lined by flowers and creeping nasturtiums. His head-gardener was the son of Octave Mirbeau's gardener, Félix Breuil.

The east section of the house. On the lawn, in spring, are « masses of daffodils ».

After moving
to Giverny,
Claude Monet
set about recreating
in his paintings
the subtle effects
of changing
sunlight
on the same subject
at various times
of day and at
different seasons.
In the « Séries »,
the principal subject
is no longer
the landscape
itself but its
changing light
and colour.

Beneath a sky
wavering between
sunshine and rain,
the azaleas
in the « Clos Normand »
on the threshold
of the Water
Lily studio

After the shower,
irises with
pearls of raindrops

29

The irises
open
more slowly
under the grey
sky of a
wet spring.
Without
the sun, these flowers
reveal their
most sumptuous
beauty which
resembles that
of the orchid.

To the no
of the proper
the cen
of the hou
showi
throu
the flow
or
sunny d

On the west side, he transformed the orchard into lawns dotted with clusters of irises and Oriental poppies and Japanese cherry and apple trees.

He had regular strips of gladioli, lark-spur, phlox, daisies, asters, etc. planted on the east side. A metal trellis along each strip was crowned with a sumptuous drapery of clematis undulating in the wind and edged a little lower down with climbing roses. The effect was delightful. The borders were adorned with rockery plants, with blue the dominant colour, and the annuals alternated with the perennials so that there were constantly some plants in flower.

Naturally, the garden changed colour each season. In spring, it was filled with daffodils followed by tulips, azaleas, rhododen-

Daylight playing
on the « Clos Normand »...

West side
at sunset.

32

drons, lilacs and wistarias and the irises which Monet loved particularly and planted in long, wide rows. Then came the tree or herbaceous peonies, gifts from his Japanese friends, followed by bellflowers, varieties of lilies, delphiniums, lupins and poppies.

In June, with the summer, came morning glories, sweet peas, bellflowers, blanket flowers, snapdragons, rose-trees in all their varieties, stocks, columbines, foxgloves, nasturtiums, phlox, gentians, sage...

September brought both single and cactus dahlias, Japanese anemones, various kinds of sunflowers, hollyhocks and asters by the hundreds...

...he house in the ...iddle of the day.

Path to the east
at sunrise

In spring, irises and
peonies in
the side
flower-beds.

Claude Monet's passionate
love of flowers
may be readily
understood
in his garden
(one of his masterpieces,
according to
his contemporaries).
«Garden-palette...
of a painter
ecstatic about flowers» ;
this is Giverny
seen by one of
the reporters
of our time who had been
invited to
the opening days
of the Claude Monet Foundation.
In this living museum,
one can stroll
about and, first, discorver the
flower-filled paths
where the painter
found his subjects,
then muse on
the fusion of reality
and an internal vision
which characterizes
the artistic method
of Monet
«the painter of light»,
as his friend,
Clemenceau,
called him.

The length
of the lawns
is broken by
several flower-beds
adorned by
old rose-trees
and poppies.

Near the house,
a poppy in the shade.

A cluster of poppies
as the sun sets.

White clematis
in the first rays of daylight.

Path on the east
side in the morning light.

In the three green-houses, Monet cultivated climbing begonias, exotic ferns and a superb collection of orchids. "After seeing Claude Monet in his garden", said Kahn in 1904, "one can understand better how a gardener of such quality became such a great painter". And Claude Monet used to say of himself : "I am good for nothing except painting and gardening".

To the west of the « Clos Normand », near the second studio, the green-houses once again play their part in creating the floral richness of the gardens.

The dazzling pallette
of colours which
the master wanted
to create
just a few steps
from his house
is now there
for visitors to see.

The Giverny Stream,
tributary of the Epte

The Water Garden. In 1893, Claude Monet bought a plot of land separated from the "Clos Normand" by the little railroad and the "chemin du Roy". After a great many complicated administrative dealings, he was finally able to have the pools dug.
Although the two sections of the property remain separate, an underpass enables visitors to wander through the whole estate. The Japanese Bridge, reconstructed today, was built in 1895.

The long-neglected
mauve wistaria
again thrusts
its way through
the railings
on the reconstructed
Japanese Bridge.

The current is fairly
strong in
the arm of
the river Epte
which supplies
water to the pool
in the
Water Garden.
Between the banks
with their
borders of
coltsfeet the light
filtering through
the flowering
cherry trees
creates the strange
effects sought
after by the
impressionist painters.

After the mauve wistaria,
the first to flower
in spring,
the white wistaria,
slower to bloom,
finally blossoms.

The Japanese Bridge
and the white
wistaria at dusk

The white
wistaria
in the clear
bright light
of evening.

To the north-east of the pool,
the mauve wistaria
of Claude Monet's time.

Nearby,
bushes of azaleas,
burberries and rhododendrons.

At the
water's edge:
irises
and poppies

The south path which begins at the Japanese Bridge and runs along the pool.

In the review, "Jardinage", 1924, Georges Truffaut described this water garden as it was in all its splendour. "The pool, whose water comes from the river Epte, is surrounded by weeping willows with golden boughs. The bed and banks are filled with a mass of plants such as heather, ferns, laurel, rhododendrons,

To the north
of the pool,
the path
is bordered
with clumps
of azaleas
and rhododendrons,
their powerful
colours contrasting
with each other.

The landing stage and
the painter's boat
seen through
the azalea bushes
on the north shore.

View
of the Water Garden
near
the Japanese Bridge.
Dotting
the surface
of the pond,
tufts
of water lilies
gradually
grow back
to the density
which characterized
the vigorous clusters
of aquatic flowers
in Monet's time.

"The whole pond
is fragrant with fresh,
young flowers
which night
has restored.
When night falls
— Monet witnessed
the scene countless
times — the young
flower retires
under the waters.
Is it not told
that its scape
calls it back
by withdrawing into
the murky depths
of the silt ?
And thus, each dawn,
the water lily...
so grand among sensitive
water plants
is reborn with
each day/a flower
forever young/
immaculate daughter
of water and sun...

...Water lilies
are summer flowers.
They are a sign
that summer
shall not fail.
When the lily
appears on the pond's
surface the cautious
gardeners take
the orange trees
out of the greenhouses.
And if in early
September the water
lily sheds its blossom,
the winter will
be hard and long.
One must rise
early and work
quickly in order
to reap,
like Monet,
the aquatic beauty
and tell the short
and passionate
ale of the river flowers."
Gaston Bachelard

The shore
of the pond

Though the stroller
often gets a glimpse
of various angles
of the water gardens
at close range,
this perspective often
disappears as
in the works
of the water
lily painter,
partially blending
into reality itself.
As was Monet's wish,
light effects
dominate on the
shores of the pond
amidst
the lush vegetation.
Flowers with
softened contours
are patches of colour
reaching out
to the atmosphere's
movements
and the endless
play of light
and shade.

azaleas and holly. The water's edges are shaded on one side by the abundant foliage of rose-trees and in the pool itself grows every known variety of water lily. On the banks, irises of several varieties are thrown into relief by tree peonies, Japanese and herbaceous peonies, clumps of cytisus and Judas trees. A large plantation of bamboos forms a thick wood. The banks also contain winter heliotropes with huge leaves on lawns of thalictrums whose leaves have been cut, certain kinds of ferns with light, downy, pink or white flowers and wistarias. There are also tamarisks and the whole garden is studded with standard and bush roses.

Between the clusters of waters lilies, all the colors of the sky are reflected on the calm surface of the pond shaded by willow trees.

The arm
of the stream
runs off
beyond the
pool towards
the fields
and the Seine.
On either
side of the
central bridge,
under the
flowering
cherry trees,
the long grass
sways
to the movement
of the
running water.

Unlike the "Clos Normand", the Water Garden is Japanese in style, asymmetrical, exotic, and lends itself to reverie in the eastern tradition of the philosophical contemplation of nature. It was a crucial factor in the work of Claude Monet.

The Water Garden as evening falls.

The banks of the pool
are filled with
the immense variety
of their former
foliage where
numerous types
of heather
alternate with lilacs,
wistarias,
cytisus, bamboos
and weeping willows.
After several
unsuccessful attempts,
the varied
layers of
water lilies
which gave birth
to the painted
universe of
the *Nymphéas*
have finally been
replanted in
the pool as they
were originally.

The famous
Japanese Bridge linking
the two banks of
the pool
at its narrowest point.
Only after 1910
were the railings
added to the bridge,
enabling the wistaria
to twine
around it,
as shown here
in the bright
morning light.

During his whole life, he would often return there to dream, inspired by the subtle interplay of light and water. It was there that he painted his first sets of Water Lilies which formed the basis of the magnificent canvases created at the very end of his life, the famous ''Décorations''. These complete the cycle of this genius's work and clearly announce the whole movement of abstract art, as Kandinsky so rightly pointed out.

The second studio, built in 1899,
has been completely restored.

It was in
this studio in
the northwest angle
of the property
that the artist
showed his works
to art dealers,
where
he signed them,
and where
he painted
the unfinished
borders of the
canvas once it
had been sold.
The studio
now features glass
bookcases
containing
Claude Monet's
books
which have
been rebound
and catalogued.
Many are
autographed
and deal
with cooking
or botany.
The building
also houses
the curator's office
and the head
gardener's
workroom.
It is not
open to
the public.

Hollyhocks against the light to the west of the Clos Normand.

The House

As in the master's time,
a cohesive harmony
is being recreated
between the house
and garden.

The house, too, has been restored. When the Académie des Beaux-Arts took over possession in 1966, the architect and member of the Académie, Jacques Carlu, was appointed curator. He immediately had the roof repaired but the interior was left without any heating due to lack of funds. In the wet climate, the furniture began to disintegrate, eaten away by fungus, the wainscoting, floors and ceiling beams rotted away, a staircase collapsed. The same happened in the second studio, opposite the green-houses, and in the water lily studio, where tree shoots began to grow.

Jacques Carlu had the master's forty-six canvases, left by his son, moved to the Musée Marmottan, where they are displayed in new surroundings. The mildewed Japanese engravings, their frames eaten into by worms, were stored in chests. The china, ceramic vases and furniture remain, as does the copperware in the kitchen.

Ten years passed before I was able, as curator of the Claude Monet Foundation, to undertake the entire restoration of all the buildings with the competent and dedicated help of Georges Luquiens, an architect from the Académie Française, thanks to Lila Acheson Wallace's donation and the wise and astute advice of her lawyer, William Barnabas McHenry. The façade of the central building was renewed. With the pink of its crushed brick surface and its green doors and shutters, it strikingly resembles an impressionist painting of the last century. It was Claude Monet who chose this green for the seats and ironwork in his garden as well as for the doors, shutters and wood on the terrace, where he often liked to sit after the evening meal.

neath
loudy sky,
façade
een
a dull
ht,
the tulips
inst a
ckground of
get-me-nots
ze with
usually vivid
es in this
en light.

In the early
1980s an old
appletree stood
here to the
east of the house,
its outline
dotted in spring
with bold red
blossoms which
contrasted with
the narcissus-
studded lawn.

The walls and furniture of the dining-room, to the right as one enters the house, have been repainted in their two slightly different shades of yellow. (This room was originally a small bedroom and kitchen). The dinner-service, of which the remaining pieces tone in with the colours in the dining-room, was ordered from Limoges. The curtains have been rewoven, the same ''blue china'' decorates the glass-doored sideboards and the

same Japanese engravings, cleaned, newly framed and identified hang in the same spots in this well-known room, remarkably full of life and memories. Claude Monet began his collection of Japanese engravings in 1871 and it could be said that he created the taste for things Japanese among the painters of his time.

The dining-room
with its décor reconstituted

His purchases show the most unerring taste; he particularly liked Utamaro, Hiroshige, Hokusaï, Toyokuni, Kiyonaga, Shunsho and Sharaku, whose works have been identified by the English art historian, David Bromfield. The generosity of Hélène David Weill made possible the restoration not only of the engravings but of all the furniture.

The ceramic tiles and copperware returned to the kitchen

Claude Monet built an extension onto his house by using the site of a small barn for his kitchen. This room was also very dilapidated. Today it gleams with the brilliance of its blue and white tiles and its restored and newly tinned copper. The stove, (which does not work), has been restored to look as it originally did, the sink, scales and weights and the sewing-machine are all there to evoke vividly middle-class life in the country at the end of the 19th century.

One of the most interesting features of the Claude Monet Foundation is the artist's collection of Japanese engravings. In addition to the dining room and drawing room on the ground floor, several rooms on the second floor have been set aside for this collection which will no doubt make up a fascinating discorvery for many visitors.

Young woman kneeling before her mosquito-lamp
HARUNOBU

A woman and her child looking at their reflection in a tub of water
UTAMARO

To the left of the front door, opposite the dining-room, is a small reading-room with its authentic furniture restored; this room opens onto a second entrance, often used by Claude Monet to go up his bedroom or to sit in his studio which he also used as a sitting-room after each meal.

On the walls, Claude Monet hung his canvases in three rows. This room, (like his bedroom on the first floor), was created on the site of a single-storey barn with a mud floor. Here, too, the past is evoked with striking authenticity, the very simple furniture is there, from his easel, cane chairs and his sofa with its sleeping china cat, (a gift from Pierre Sicard), to the hemp carpet, cleaned and renewed.

The small reading-room restored

Gérard Delorme has generously made a gift of these paintings, identical replicas of the master's works, created by means of his new process of reproduction in colour and relief. They bring life and vitality to the walls of this studio.

On the floor above the studio is the master's bedroom; it was

The drawing-room/studio in the west section of the house

here that he slept from 1883 to 1926; here, too, that he died. All the furniture still exists, including a superb 18th century marquetry writing-desk and a very fine antique chest-of-drawers. The fabrics on the walls and arm-chairs have been

rewoven. Beside this room is his wash-room, that of Alice his
wife, and her bedroom. On the other side of the central staircase
were the children's bedrooms and, in the attic, those of the
servants. It was in his bedroom and the adjoining rooms that
Claude Monet kept the collection that he liked to show his
friends. It was here, too, that he hung the paintings he had
bought from or had been given by painters whose talent he held
in esteem. Among them were twelve Cézannes, including "Le
Nègre Scipion", a portrait of Claude Monet and his wife, another
portrait of Madame Monet reading "Le Figaro", two nudes and
"The Kasbah of Algiers", all by Renoir; eight Manets, five Berthe
Morisots, two Degas, three Delacroix, a Fantin-Latour, several
Pissarros, a Signac, a Vuillard, "Rain", by Caillebotte, four
Jongkinds, two Rodin bronzes...
A magnificent collection now scattered throughout various
museums in all parts of the world.

The Water Lily Studio

It was built in 1916, (on the site of a tumble-down cottage), so that Monet could paint at ease and in good light the great "Décorations des Nymphéas", the finest set of which the master gave to France in 1922 at Georges Clemenceau's instigation. This is therefore the cradle of his artistic legacy. In very bad condition, this studio was restored at great expense thanks to Michel David Weill's two generous donations. The easels, several mobile trestles and the sofa are still here, and the walls are decorated with magnificent reproductions, gifts from Gérard Delorme, of Monet's large format paintings.

Claude Monet
in the Water Lily studio
around 1920

The visitor enters the informal world of Giverny's master through the vast Water Lily studio which basks in the vertical lighting which gave birth to the famous "Décorations". The great canvases dealing with the Water Garden were in fact created in this studio, and not on the shores of the pond. After having seen the rest of the Foundation the visitor will cross the Water Lily studio once again where a substantial amount of documents are on display.

At long last this task, unique in France, has been accomplished : the house and gardens of an artist known throughout the world have been recreated with the greatest care and authenticity in untouched surroundings. There is no doubt that this effort will meet with great public acclaim.

ach morning,
hen the clear darkness
f a summer's night
ades away,
ne petals
f the water
owers part.
he lilies bloom
ith the brightness
f midday,
nen slowly close
nce again when
usk shrouds
ne pond
n darkness.

"So much youth
again and again
so faithfully submissive
to the rythm of
day and night
so punctual
in sounding
the break of dawn
this is why
the water lily
encompasses
impressionism.
The water lily
is one of
the world's moments.
It is morning
to our eyes.
It is the
astonishing flower of
a summer's dawn."
Gaston Bachelard

Giverny's donors

Through the generosity of Mrs Lila Acheson Wallace, the Académie Française was able to purchase the farm opposite the Foundation and a vast plot of ground which has been made into a parking area. We have, thanks to this purchase been able to install offices for the Head Gardener, living accomodations for volunteer assistants, and apartments and studios which are reserved for three young American artists. These artists are selected through a contest and invited each year by reader's Digest to paint at Giverny from April to November.

"The Versailles Foundation is tax deductible for United States citizens".
The following organizations are authorized to accept your donations :

Société des Amis de Claude Monet
Président M. Toulgouat
27260 GIVERNY

Versailles Foundation
Présidente Mme Van der Kemp
420, Lexington avenue, Graybar building
NEW YORK CITY N.Y. 10170

The Foundation is open daily from 10.00 a.m. to 6 p.m., except Mondays, from April 1st until October 31st.